How Not to Become a Crotchety Old Man

How NOT
to Become
a Crotchety
Old Man

Mary McHugh
Illustrations by Adrienne Hartman

Andrews McMeel
PUBLISHING®

Andrews McMeel Publishing
a division of Andrews McMeel Universal
1130 Walnut Street, Kansas City, Missouri 64106
www.andrewsmcmeel.com

17 18 19 20 21 WKT 13 12 11 10 9 8

ISBN: 978-0-7407-8155-1
Library of Congress Control Number: 2008937973

Illustrations copyright © 2004 by Adrienne Hartman

ATTENTION: SCHOOLS AND BUSINESSES
Andrews McMeel books are available at quantity discounts
with bulk purchase for educational, business, or sales
promotional use. For information, please e-mail the
Andrews McMeel Publishing Special Sales Department:
specialsales@amuniversal.com.

Introduction

Crotchety Old Men are everywhere: on the road crouched behind the wheels of old gas guzzlers; at home whining because they can't find their glasses, keys, or wallets; stomping around grocery stores grumbling that they don't sell any decent food anymore; and bent over their morning newspapers foaming at the mouth at the most recent outrages committed by politicians.

We all have Crotchety Old Men in our lives. Your Crotchety Old Man could be your father, your grandfather, your older brother, your husband, or even—*you!* Crotchety Old Men can easily be identified by remarks such as "What's this white stuff all over my meat?" and "If they don't stop sending money to all those foreign places, this country will be bankrupt in five years!" If you even suspect you might be one or if you're sure that you're living with one, you will recognize the following signs.

Crotchety Old Men...

Should never wear Speedos.

Don't like to eat
"stuff covered with
white sauce."

4

Don't want to even *hear* the word "menopause."

5

Actually like prunes.

Think women were born
to clean—like their mothers.

Love cordless drills as gifts—
no one knows why.

Believe "You look OK"
is a compliment.

7

Think women were
invented to look pretty
and have children.

8

Never learned to put a
new roll of toilet paper
on the rod.

9

Wish women would just
shut up and let them talk.

Wish somebody would
do something about
Hillary Clinton.

12

Believe women aren't smart
enough to be lawyers, doctors,
or investment brokers.

Think everybody else
should get off the road
when they're driving.

14

Think we should ship all immigrants back where they came from.

Forget what foreplay means,
if they ever knew.

Become couch potatoes
during football season.

Believe they were
born to be waited on.

Think throwing a steak
on the grill is cooking.

Never get through a day
without asking at least once,
"Where's my (glasses,
keys, papers, etc.)?"

Still laugh at Abbott
and Costello.

Don't understand why they have to put the toilet seat down.

21

Think the clothes they throw
on the floor just magically
end up in the hamper.

Don't know how to take things
out of the dishwasher and
put them away.

Grumble that no one looks
like them, sounds like them,
eats like them, or behaves
properly anymore.

Can cure anyone's insomnia
by talking about bird watching,
stamp collecting, or
baseball statistics.

Love to explain things
you've known for years.

Think money should be
spent on beer, golf,
and baseball games.

Truly believe women
thought up crying just
to get their own way.

Consider the silent treatment
from their wives a reward.

Think "weekend"
means "sports."

Look upon belching
as an art form.

Think "sensitive man" is
the same thing as "wimp."

Exercise only when the batteries in the TV remote control are dead and they have to get up to change channels.

Forget anniversaries and birthdays but remember the day their golf score first broke 100.

Consider white wine
a sissy drink.

34

Salt everything automatically
before tasting it.

35

Like guns even
better than naps.

Think they look
great in caps.

Think most people
are stupid.

Think only sissies
say, "I love you."

Announce at dinner parties that a woman's place is in the house, not the House.

Think women should be
banned from the golf course
and should have a separate
entrance into the dining room.

Haven't been awake to see in the New Year since 1948.

Prefer women who agree with everything they say.

Wish John Wayne
would come back.

Suspect anyone with
facial hair of being a terrorist.

Never let a day go by without complaining about *something*.

Expect women in their office—
and home—to make coffee.

Still act the way they
did in high school.

Hate every present
you give them.

Think movies are a total
waste of money.

A woman was married to a Crotchety Old Man who always said to her, "When I die, I want you to bury all my money with me. Promise me that." She promised and when the man finally died, a friend asked if she kept her promise. "Oh yes," she said. "I wrote him a check."

Can't remember anything but the name of some football player from the '20s, and say, "I've got a remarkable memory."

Refer to anyone who has an opinion different from theirs as a "commie-pinko simp."

Think a good way to start
a conversation is "What did
you do in World War II?"

Think if they scramble an egg
for themselves they should
be given a medal.

Think Mother's Day and Valentine's Day are fake holidays to get people to spend money.

Remember when a home cost $13,000, and brag about how much their house is worth now sixty years later.

Remember when they could
replace parts in appliances
and refuse to buy new ones.

Won't turn their hearing aid
on because "there's too much
noise in here!"

Think there hasn't been
a good war since
World War II.

Consider the words
"male chauvinist pig"
as a compliment.

Stand in the middle
of the kitchen and say,
"Where's the butter?"

Think vegetarians
are nutcases.

Are sure their wives spend
money just to annoy them.

Say things like:
"Kids today have it too easy."

Don't think there has been a
good comedian since Jack Benny.

Are convinced that people who want to save the whales belong in the loony bin.

Hope everyone at a
peace demonstration
will be arrested.

Don't understand why everyone
doesn't agree with them.

Think men who cry
should get over it.

Hate small talk and
think most talk *is* small

Keep saying, "Speak up!
Don't mumble!"

Think they should be
praised loudly when they
do a load of wash.

Think when they forget something, it's normal, but when their wives forget something, it's Alzheimer's.

Lose their sense of taste as they get older and blame it on their wives' cooking.

Think the proper present
for a wife is another bathrobe.

Grow hair everywhere
but on their heads.

Take it personally when
the Dow Jones goes down

Love to say, "You don't know
what you're talking about."

Don't think anybody can
tell they have combed
their hair over their
bald heads.

Don't understand
African-American names
and think they should all
be called Mary or John.

Consider hardware stores the only ones worth shopping in.

Start off each day with
a complaint about
the weather, the news,
the neighbors,
breakfast, everything.

Won't travel to other countries because, "I haven't seen all of America yet."

Love dumb-blonde jokes.

Remember when you took a job with a company out of college and stayed with them until you were sixty-five and then retired and moved to Florida.

Fall asleep in their chair after lunch, before dinner, and after dinner, and wonder why they can't get to sleep at night.

Don't see anything wrong with calling a woman "a broad."

Walk in the middle of the sidewalk and expect everyone to get out of the way.

Love Rush Limbaugh.
Hate Tom Brokaw.

Leave the room when women
talk about their pregnancies
or menopause.

Yell at anchormen and
women on newscasts.

Drink *real* coffee and then
stay awake all night.

Think food is supposed to be
meat and potatoes, not salads.

Have no idea who half the
people on *Charlie Rose* are.

Do not understand
Adam Sandler at *all*.

Hate twenty-four-hour-a-day news channels. "Twice a day is enough."

Don't understand people
who don't eat butter,
cream, and eggs.

Love Polish jokes and don't understand why no one tells them anymore.

Refuse to open the windows
in winter because, "You're
heating the whole outdoors."

Say, "Where did you
hide my socks?"

Think complimenting
their wives will spoil them.

Only read books about
presidents and wars.

Look upon Home Depot
as a place of worship.

Think everybody's nice until
you get to know them.

Think all New Age stuff is
one more sign the world
is going to hell.

Consider golf the perfect game because, "There are no women allowed in our club."

Think the funniest scene in any movie *ever* is the farting scene in *Blazing Saddles*.

Always sound as if
they're mad at something
even when they aren't.

Don't mind dogs but expect
their wives to walk them.

Don't really trust the Japanese
because of Pearl Harbor.

Think only gay people
have AIDS.

Hate the French—
but then, who doesn't?

Do not approve of female cops, firemen, or soldiers, and barely put up with women doctors and lawyers.

Accept their own paunches
but think their wives should
exercise to get rid of
their tummies.

Do not understand *Seinfeld.*
"Who *are* these people?"

Take mealtimes *very* seriously.

Think Eminem is a candy.

Pretend they read *Playboy* for the articles.

Think the perfect death would be
in the middle of a golf game
with their cleats on.

Always read the obituary page
first to make sure they're
not in there.

Don't mind being a grandfather
so much, but they hate being
married to a grandmother.

Like babies—when they
are in another room.

Think they deserve a medal
for taking out the trash.

Think everyone in this country should speak English.

Think wrestling is a legitimate sport.

Never understood that women
don't like to be called "dearie,"
as in "That too complicated
for you, dearie?"

Remember when gas cost
ten cents a gallon and tell you
about it every time they
fill up their tanks.

Expect somebody else
to answer the phone.

A Crotchety Old Man decided to wash his sweatshirt. He threw it in the washing machine and yelled to his wife, "What setting do I use?" "What does it say on the shirt?" his wife asked. He yelled back, "University of Texas."

Think the way to solve international problems is to bomb the hell out of them.

Go to doctors as a hobby.

Blame everyone but themselves
when things go wrong.

Think it's funny to ask little kids,
"How's your childhood going?"

Say, "The world has gone
to hell in a handbasket."

Think homeless people are just lazy and could get off the streets if they really tried.

Think Casual Fridays are
proof that the business world
has lost its mind.

Think young girls don't wear
enough clothes these days.

Take it personally if people don't return their calls IMMEDIATELY.

Watch sexy ladies exercising on TV and change the channel when someone comes in the room.

Can have lunch with an old friend and not ask "How's your wife?" or "What are your children doing now?"

Have mouths that have
turned down at the corners
for so long you can't tell
when they're smiling.

Get shorter but refuse
to admit it.

Hibernate in winter.

Laugh at their own jokes.

Don't laugh at anyone
else's jokes.

Refuse to go anywhere
during football season.

Still ask, "What kind
of name is that?"

Glacial melt swamps Paris!

Nevada becomes beach front (?)

Believe global warming is
nonsense thought up by
the "touchy-feelies."

Say things like: "Nobody knows how to make a decent pot roast anymore."

Think pigs in a blanket is
not only the best hors d'oeuvre,
but would make a great dinner.

Leave their keys in the
bird feeder, the space heater,
and the refrigerator.

Cheat on their diets but yell
at their wives when they
eat one M&M.

Will never believe one line
in this book is about them.